THE BOOK OF MOE

THE SIMPSONS™ LIBRARY OF WISDOM
THE BOOK OF MOE

Copyright © 2008 by
Matt Groening Productions, Inc. All rights reserved.

HarperCollins*Publishers*
77—85 Fulham Palace Road
Hammersmith, London W6 8JB
www.harpercollins.co.uk

Published by HarperCollins 2008

FIRST EDITION
ISBN-13: 978-0-00-726708-8
ISBN-10: 0-00-726708-8

3 5 7 9 10 8 6 4 2

Publisher: Matt Groening
Creative Director: Bill Morrison
Managing Editor: Terry Delegeane
Director of Operations: Robert Zaugh
Art Director: Nathan Kane
Special Projects Art Director: Serban Cristescu
Production Manager: Christopher Ungar
Assistant Art Director: Chia-Hsien Jason Ho
Production/Design: Karen Bates, Art Villanueva
Staff Artists: Mike Rote
Production Assistant: Nathan Hamill
Administration: Sherri Smith
Legal Guardian: Susan A. Grode

THE SIMPSONS™ LIBRARY OF WISDOM

Conceived and Edited by Bill Morrison
Book Design, Art Direction, and Production by Serban Cristescu
Contributing Editor: Terry Delegeane

HarperCollins Editors: Hope Innelli and Jeremy Cesarec

Contributing Artists: MARCOS ASPREC, KAREN BATES, DARREL BOWEN, JOHN COSTANZA,
SERBAN CRISTESCU, DAN DAVIS, MIKE DECARLO, JOHN DELANEY, PETE GOMEZ, NATHAN HAMILL,
NATHAN KANE, JAMES LLOYD, SCOTT MCRAE, BILL MORRISON, KIMBERLY NARSETE, KEVIN M. NEWMAN,
JOEY NILGES, MIKE ROTE, ROBERT STANLEY, STEVE STEERE JR., ERICK TRAN, ART VILLANUEVA

Contributing Writers: TERRY DELEGEANE, SCOTT M. GIMPLE, AMANDA MCCANN, JESSE LEON MCCANN,
BILL MORRISON, ERIC ROGERS, MARY TRAINOR, PATRIC M. VERRONE

Special Thanks to:
Pete Benson, N. Vyolet Diaz, Deanna MacLellan, Helio Salvatierra, Mili Smythe, and Ursula Wendel

Manufactured in China

THE BOOK OF MOE

HARPER

NEW YORK • LONDON • TORONTO • SYDNEY

Moe's Top Forty

1. BOXING KANGAROOS.
2. TEXAS NO-PANTS POKER.
3. THE LEFTORIUM.
4. MAGGIE SIMPSON.
5. MAGGIE'S MOMMY MIDGE.
6. MR. SNOOKUMS.
7. JAMES BROWN.
8. PICKLES IN JARS.
9. PRIDE.
10. PREJUDICE.
11. PROZAC™.
12. THE RAT PACK.
13. PACK RATS.
14. PAYBACKS.
15. BOWLING.
16. PROWLING.
17. LURKING.
18. SKULKING.
19. EDITH PIAF.

20. CHARLES BUKOWSKI.
21. JACQUELINE KENNEDY ONASSIS.
22. HAI KARATE COLOGNE FOR MEN.
23. A DRY BAR TOWEL.
24. CLAMP-ON WIGS.
25. OFF-TRACK BETTING.
26. BOILERMAKERS.
27. FIXING A FIGHT.
28. THROWING A GAME.
29. THE FREE TRADE OF EXOTIC ANIMALS UNHINDERED BY GOVERNMENT-IMPOSED TARIFFS.
30. STALKING A DAME.
31. FLUFFY KITTENS.
32. THE MOVEMENTARIANS.
33. CLIP-ON TIES.
34. BOOZEHOUNDS.
35. MARIO PUZO.
36. CALLER ID.
37. BAR FLIES.
38. ASPIRIN.
39. WASHER/DRYER DRAG RACES.
40. TAKING THE LAW INTO YOUR OWN HANDS.

A DAY IN THE LIFE OF MOE

7:00 A.M. Wakes to what will be the MOST DEPRESSING day of his life, although it begins like any other—with him contemplating suicide.

7:10 A.M. His breakfast cereal does not stay crunchy in milk.

7:20 A.M. While laying out clothes to wear, cannot find matching black socks. Spray paints blue one black.

7:25 A.M. Finds notice slipped under door. Neighbors have signed petition. All agree he stinks.

7:30 A.M. Stands in bathwater, ready to drop plugged-in radio/says good-bye to lonely, cruel, unyielding universe.

7:32 A.M. Before he can drop radio, he hears terrible news: CRABBY (Concerned Retirees Against Booze, Bartenders, and Yodelers) to rally today. Bunch of old people protesting booze/bartenders is bad enough, but he just started yodeling classes!

7:45 A.M. Much too mad to think about suicide, he sits in tepid bathwater/growls at cockroach climbing on soap.

8:00 A.M. Opens bar for before-work crowd. Strangely, no one comes in. Not even Barney. Feeling of dread forms/hangs over his head like "freakin' sword of Damocles."

8:35 A.M. Television news reports overturned beer truck on interstate caused by CRABBY protesters shuffling in/out of traffic. Barney featured cavorting naked in beer spouts. That explains where all his morning alkies are.

9:00 A.M. Kent Brockman's Morning Trivia Challenge on TV: "What are the main ingredients in a Singapore Sling cocktail?" First caller with correct answer wins free tickets for Duff Blimp ride. Moe actually knows answer/excitedly reaches for phone.

9:01 A.M. Phone rings just before he picks it up. Incoming call for "Ophelia Bottom from Lake Titicaca." Justifiably thinks it is a prank call. Threatens to rip off caller's ears/stuff them up caller's "snot holes." Caller promises to come down/bust Moe in his own snot holes. Tells caller to bring baseball, because Moe's got his bat.

9:02 A.M. Hangs up/false sense of superiority disappears when he hears TV announce that no one has called in to answer Trivia Challenge. Duff Blimp tickets will be given to kids at Springfield Children's Orphanage for the Adorably Sad.

9:30 A.M. Closes tavern until later. As he walks to his car, he is spotted by angry CRABBY protesters. Hops in his car/easily outruns electric scooters/walkers, only to discover his Slim Whitman records in backseat smashed/tires deflated.

10:00 A.M. Walks to soup kitchen to finish reading book to homeless. Today: the stunning conclusion of "The Da Vinci Code." As he reads, he is suddenly shocked to discover last twenty pages of book ripped out. Pretends to read/improvises ending based on movie he saw once about Da Vinci.

10:30 A.M. Smelly vagrant/ex-movie reviewer reveals Moe faking "The Da Vinci Code" ending/adding scenes from old movie "Three Stooges vs. Da Vinci." Moe escapes angry homeless mob/is pelted by shoes, spoons, wooden crosses, tepid bowls of soup of the day.

10:45 A.M. Staggers to nearby park/lays down under tree/rests head against trunk. Looks like depressed Charlie Brown...albeit ugly/troll-like.

11:00 A.M. Officers Lou/Eddie approach on park patrol/arrest Moe for vagrancy/possible squirrel abuse.

11:30 A.M. Joins naked, sloppily sentimental Barney in slammer. Hugged repeatedly, he tries to escape down toilet.

12:00 P.M. Released with citations for loitering/impersonating "Peanuts" character. Chief Wiggum allows Barney to leave wearing police uniform, as long as he promises to return it very soon.

12:30 P.M. Returns to tavern to find it blockaded by unruly CRABBY protesters. Barney attempts to disband seniors with new cop powers. Rebellious cane swinging ensues.

12:45 P.M. Sneaks into tavern through ground-level cellar window/shreds best bow tie on broken glass.

12:50 P.M. Distressed to discover shipment of piranhas in plastic bag has sprung a leak. Fears huge smuggling profit loss!

1:00 P.M. CRABBY has turned off tavern's water, so Moe cannot fill another plastic bag. He relocates piranhas to Men's Room toilet bowl.

1:15 P.M. Opens delivery received yesterday/discovers incorrect shipment of booze—instead of one case of 151 rum, he received 151 cases of regular rum. Also, real umbrellas instead of frou-frou umbrellas for mixed drinks. Lots of forehead slapping follows.

1:30 P.M. Barflies Sam/Larry fight their way into bar/carrying in wounded Barney. While Moe screams at bar supply company on phone, Larry pours rum on Barney's open lacerations. Barney pours three bottles of rum down throat.

1:35 P.M. Moe realizes excessive rum wasting taking place/has conniption. Colossal tug-of-war worthy of Keystone Cops movie develops.

2:00 P.M. Cursing/disgusted Moe mops up pools of rum. Throws booze-soaked bar towels/Barney in corner.

2:30 P.M. Group of dames come in/order tropical cocktails. They flee after Moe tries to put real umbrellas in their drinks/smelly, drunken cop breathes on them.

3:00 P.M. Tavern-goers willing to cross CRABBY picket line begin to fill the bar.

3:30 P.M. Incoming call for "LeDum, first name Uri." Moe calls out "Uri LeDum! Do you know Uri LeDum? I'm saying Uri LeDum!" Glares/jeering laughter follow. Threatens to sew caller's lips to fire hose/turn on hydrant.

4:00 P.M. Shocking Kent Brockman report on TV: Protesters threatening to tear down beloved Roy Roger's Yodeling Cowboy Museum on next block. Declaring he's had enough, Moe grabs shotgun/promises to "rock salt their world!"

4:15 P.M. Infuriated by sight of old folks pulling at museum walls with cables attached to power wheelchairs, Moe fires warning shot into air. Unfortunately, shot punctures Duff Blimp directly overhead. Sounds of shock/horror/adorably sad orphan screams fill air as deflating blimp loses altitude.

4:25 P.M. Aged protesters unable to get out of airship's

path, even though Duff Blimp drifts to ground ten minutes after being perforated. Pandemonium!

4:45 P.M. CRABBY members regroup, identify Moe as bartender/blimp killer. Soon they have Moe boxed in. As angry elders advance on him, wheezing furiously, Moe fears these may be his last moments on Earth.

5:00 P.M. Senior citizens break for dinner. Moe is saved.

5:15 P.M. Grateful that one lucky thing has finally happened today, Moe heads back to tavern. Suddenly, his way is blocked by huge, brick wall of a man who tosses baseball up into air/ominously mentions Lake Titicaca. Moe gets punched repeatedly in snot holes.

6:00 P.M. Back at bar, Moe licks his wounds. Barely listens as Lenny/Carl advise him on how to save damaged nose cartilage.

6:30 P.M. Cheers up slightly when he sells fat cigar to Homer Simpson. Tells him it's Cuban. Loosely speaking, it is—it is made from rolled-up Cuban newspapers.

7:00 P.M. It is only when Homer quickly lurches for Men's Room that Moe remembers that his "Cubans" have certain laxative-like properties.

7:02 P.M. Homer runs out of Men's Room with pants down/several piranhas clamped onto his butt. He makes two complete circles around bar, trailing thick smoke from his smoldering stogie, screams piercingly/drops cigar onto pile of rum-soaked towels/Barney on floor.

8:00 P.M. Moe's Tavern is completely engulfed in flames. Volunteer firefighters arrive thirty minutes too late—mainly because they were all drinking at Moe's bar when the fire started/had to go get the fire truck.

8:30 P.M. Moe sits on ash-covered curb across street from charred wooden frame of what was once his tavern: some say he sobbed, while others defend Moe's dignity and say it was "hot cinders in his eyes."

Then one kid wearing a vest rides by on bike/makes everything worse by shouting, "Haw haw!"

8:45 to 11:40 P.M. Next few hours are hazy. Only remembers repeatedly punching self in gut/rending his clothing/chewing on blacktop.

11:45 P.M. Marge Simpson pulls up to find Moe lying prone in street in pool of his own tears. She quickly scoots him into car/explains that Maggie is teething. Moe's the only one who can calm Maggie when she is like this.

12:01 A.M. A new day begins/finds Moe in rocking chair with Maggie in his arms. He quietly yodels Maggie to sleep with his croaking, froggy voice. As Maggie's soothing breaths lull him to sleep, Moe thinks, "Life is good."

THANKS, MOE! Sober Advice

to the Somewhat Inebriated

POETRY IN MOE-TION

New poems from the writer of the modern-day epic poem "Howling at a Concrete Moon" as seen in the pages of *American Poetry Perspectives*.

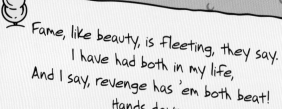

Fame, like beauty, is fleeting, they say.
I have had both in my life,
And I say, revenge has 'em both beat!
Hands down.
Oooh...and chasing some deadbeat rummy out
of your bar with a double-barreled shotgun.
That's good, too.

Pickled eggs.
You sit there on the counter, next to the cash register.
Your brine is murky, smelly, and antiseptic.
Your presence calms me.
I'd sacrifice any one of these knuckle-headed barflies—
Stick a knife into any one of 'em and gut 'em right here on the bar
To keep you happy.
Pickled eggs.

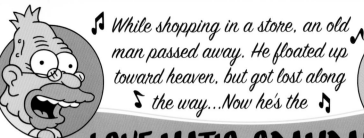

LOVE-MATIC GRAMPA!

♪ While shopping in a store, an old man passed away. He floated up toward heaven, but got lost along the way...Now he's the ♪

MAYBE I LOST MY CHARM, LOVE TESTER. I AIN'T DONE A BROAD IN I DON'T KNOW *HOW* LONG...

YOU WANT *MY* ADVICE?

SURE...

"NEVER TAKE ADVICE FROM A HAUNTED ARCADE NOVELTY MACHINE!"

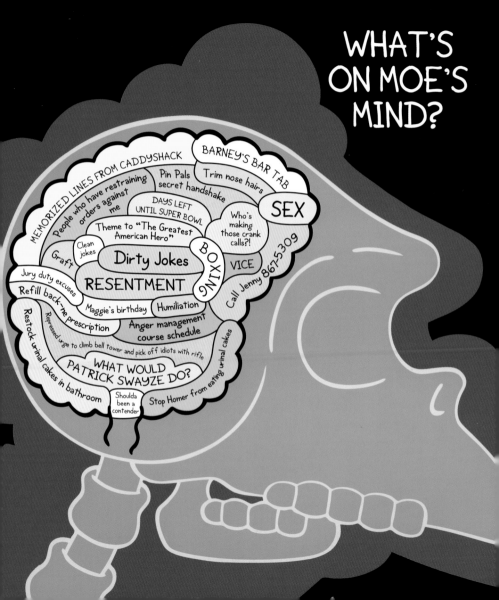

ANATOMY OF MOE

THE 'DO
Sold after each haircut to a company that makes scouring pads.

LISTENIN' HOLES
Versatile. Often hears "maybe" when a woman says "no."

YAPPER
Dispenser of advice for drunks and purveyor of off-color jokes.

SHIRT POCKET
Contents: an I.O.U. from C. U. Latersucker.

CLIP-ON BOW TIE
Shows the patrons he runs a classy establishment on par with his competitors "T.G.I. Boobies," "Juggernauts," and "Nipplebee's Neighborhood Bar & Grille."

EMPTY POCKET
Reserved for tips.

KEISTER
Flat in appearance, except for a thick wallet and a couple of handkerchiefs.

DOGS
Cursed with the uniquely revolting aroma of baby barf, blue cheese, and smoking brake pads.

BRAIN BUCKET
Thick, according to any woman who's asked him to get something through it.

PEEPERS
Always peeled to prevent theft from the pickled egg jar.

BEEZER
Pugnacious from numerous prize fights. Able to sniff out bad tippers and soiled diapers from 50 yards out.

LOVE MUSCLE
Broken too many times to count on 8 fingers, but still open to finding his one true love—or at least someone crazy or drunk enough to say "I do."

MITTS
"Duff Book of World Records" holder for "Sweatiest Palms."

MEAT HOOKS
Nimble, yet strong. Excellent for gripping a baseball bat or squeezing a shotgun trigger.

DIRTY BAR RAG
Last washed in 1992.

KNEECAPS
Knobby from years of begging and pleading with women and loan sharks.

APRON
Constantly soaked with beer suds, conversation spittle, palm sweat, and bar food grease.

THE MYSTERY OF
Just where the heck did

HEY, I'M A *BEEFEATER!* SO...WHERE'S THE *BEEF*?

LOOK AT ME! I'M THE *OTHER* MARX BROTHER... *GAUCHO!*

I CRUISE THE SINGLES BARS, LOOKIN' FOR A *CZECH-MATE!*

ENGLAND?

ARGENTINA?

CZECHOSLOVAKIA?

YA KNOW, IT TAKES A LOTTA GUTS TO FIGHT IN A *MINISKIRT!*

IN THE OLD DAYS, POLE DANCER MEANT SOMETHIN' *COMPLETELY* DIFFERENT!

WHAT'S A GRECIAN URN? ...ABOUT $8.50 AN HOUR!

HAH! I NEVER GET TIRED OF THAT ONE.

ITALY?

POLAND?

GREECE?

MEMORIES OF MOE
a photo album
by Moe Szyslak

You could say I was born into the bartendin' biz. My pop used to put a dash of bourbon in my bottle every night. Knowin' Ma, I woulda consumed more alcohol if I'd been breast-fed.

This is the last picture taken of my pop smilin'. My mother left him three days later for a member of the Jimmy Dorsey Orchestra. Pop cried himself to sleep to "Green Eyes" every night. Helen O'Connell took exception to Ma and kicked her off the band bus in Poughkeepsie.

My first tavern. These guys still have an unpaid lemonade and Pez tab.

The day I graduated from bartendin' school. Pop was so proud a' me...ya sorta had to be there.

This was the day I opened my bar. A very lethal game of rock, paper, scissors broke out before last call. You wouldn't have believed the blood...we don't talk much about that no more.

Boy, this was a game no one will ever forget. The Isotopes ended their season 0-for-162, and we didn't have to watch 'em again for a whole six months. Lousy bums...god, I love 'em.

If I ever find that prank-happy little twerp that's always callin' my bar, I'll be sure to introduce him to Bart Simpson, so he can see how a good kid treats his elders!

You know what I love most about the holidays? The traditions.

My vacation. A word of caution: Jamaica, Queens, ain't nothin' like the real Jamaica!

Sick kids. I'd give 'em all a big hug if I could, but God only knows what diseases they're spreading through their little hands and mouths. So I just read to 'em from a safe, sterile-like distance. It ain't easy bein' such a giver.

My second true love, although she never knew it.

That's me and Renee, my first true love. I feel like she broke my heart into a million little pieces, vacuumed the bits up, removed the vacuum bag, tossed it into a volcano, and then the volcano got hit by an atomic bomb...but that's the way love goes, right?

I simply call this one... Midge.

My friends. They're the best. Especially after closing time or whenever they pay their tabs...or any money at all for that matter. Lousy, stinkin', no-good, freeloadin'...

WHATEVER HAPPENED TO WHAT'S-HIS-NAME? THE WHO'S WHO OF HOLLYWOOD HAS-BEENS

Moe "Smelly" Szyslak—The least known of "The Little Rascals"

Career Low-Lights:
- Born Morris Szyslak in Indiana.
- After reading that Shirley Temple was pulling down a sweet three grand a week, Mrs. Szyslak packs up seven-year-old Moe and moves to Hollywood.
- Producer Hal Roach catches wind of Moe and casts him in the role of the lice-infested kid named Smelly in the long-running series "The Little Rascals."
- Audiences find both the character and the actor repugnant.
- Smelly is dropped after only four episodes and replaced by a mangy dog called Scuzzy.

- Changing his name to "Snot-nosed Moe from Kokomo" does little to endear him to studio execs.
- Goes from obscurity at age seven to oblivion by age seven and a half.
- Sues his mother for his wages—is awarded one hundred dollars that he spends on candy bars and cigarettes.
- Pleads no contest to punching an autograph seeker who mistook him for someone famous.
- Studio quashes Moe's attempt to open a theme park named Smellville.
- Former costar Irving "Fatso" Mervyn bails Moe out of jail after he's arrested for shoplifting candy bars and cigarettes.
- Studio nixes Moe's plan to package Smelly's trademark aroma as men's cologne.
- Joins the Navy and gets stationed, ironically, in Kokomo.
- Has a brief, undistinguished stint as a boxer.
- Opens a bar in Springfield.
- Reappears on television as the surprisingly handsome Dr. Tad Winslow on the soap opera "It Never Ends."
- Fired from the show after both revealing top-secret plot lines on live TV and falling victim to a career-ending scenery malfunction.
- Currently living out his days in quiet desperation.

MOE "SMELLY" SZYSLAK

MOE "SMELLY" SZYSLAK

Moe "Smelly" Szyslak's official police mug shot.

Appeared as Smelly in the following "Little Rascals" episodes:

"Somethin' Sure Do Smells"
"Soap Is for Sissies"
"I Ain't in Need o' No Skoolin'"
"Die, You Nazi Bastards!"

Title card from Smelly's debut film.

Trivia:

- Smelly's signature catchphrase was: "What are you lookin' at, pervert?"

Moe "Smelly" Szyslak's official publicity head shot.

Szyslak and Irving "Fatso" Mervyn in a scene from "Soap Is for Sissies."

- Moe originally created the classic "car exhaust soot-in-the-face" bit now performed regularly by "Krusty the Clown Show" cast member Sideshow Mel.
- Before the filming of each scene, Mrs. Szyslak would hiss, "Twinkle, little star! Twinkle!" to her son.
- Rumors still persist that the studio publicity machine covered up for Moe after he killed fellow Rascal Alfalfa for stealing his "car exhaust soot-in-the-face" bit.

Personal Quotes:

- "Hollywood chewed me up and spit me out like a saliva-soaked wad of chaw tobacco."
- "I was just one more wide-eyed chump they put through the dream factory sausage grinder and then tossed out like yesterday's garbage."
- "Them show biz creeps kicked me to the curb like I was a pile of stinkin' dog-doo."
- "I was washed up by the time I was in third grade."
- "'So long, sucker!' they says. 'Don't let the stage door hit you on the friggin' keister on your way out.'"
- "Bitter? Who...me?!"

ASK MOE

Q: A guy at the office is always hogging the microwave at lunch, making blintzes. By the time he's finished, lunch hour is over, and I'm left with a can of uncooked chili. He's always there before me, and when I've asked him if I could use the micro first, he just laughs at me. What can I do?

A: Get in the office real early, I'm sayin' like at the crack of butt. Tape paper clips inside the microwave. When blintz-boy makes his high-class lunch, he's gonna wind up with a nice li'l side order of radioactive explosion in the face. When he's stumblin' 'round the kitchen with his hair on fire, beat him with the toaster. Or, if you don't want to go to all that trouble, go out for lunch. Or try that Krusty's self-heatin' chili with the sterno right in the can. Either way's good.

Q: I love my girlfriend, but she doesn't have her own car, and she's always borrowing mine. What can I do to get her to find her own wheels?

A: My policy is, if you don't have to actually pay your girlfriend for bein' your girlfriend, you're way ahead of the game. Let her borrow your car, you idiot. On a side note, I'm so very lonely.

Q: I'm not very athletic, but I join my chums for softball every week—for the camaraderie and the simple, visceral pleasures that organized sport provides. Last week, at the bottom of the ninth, with two outs for our side, it fell upon me to win the game. Alas, my skills were lacking, and I struck out. Since then, the fellows' teasing has been incessant. What can I do to stop my friends from ridiculing me?

A: Let me tell you a little story. There was once this college-boy-nancy-pants who wanted to play ball with the real guys and then lost the big game. Then he wrote me a letter, and it made me want to punch him in the mouth. Learn to be a man and hit the clutch ball. Until then, be lucky insults are the only thing bein' thrown your way. Me, I woulda gone with Duff bottles filled with fire ants.

Q: My girlfriend and I have a great relationship, but she always gets mad that I never cry at the movies. She thinks I have a heart of stone when it comes to romance. Help!

A: Cryin' at movies is strictly for women or people with eye problems (unless you're watchin' "The Champ," 'cuz that movie is just...well...I mean, why'd he have to DIE? Right? But part of bein' a man is trickin' your lady into thinkin' your heart isn't a black, cold lump of nuthin', and you actually have some feelings coursin' through your brains and veins. So do this: before you step into the theater, secretly smash your hand in the car door.

THE TRUTH IS UGLY. THE GUY WHO SPEAKS THE TRUTH IS UGLIER.

It'll keep you cryin' from the trailers to the end credits. After the show, make some excuse like you gotta go puke from sadness and immediately seek medical assistance so you don't wind up with a hook.

Q: I bought a car off an old pal who was in some financial trouble and it turned out to be a real lemon. One day, all the wheels just fell off and the air conditioner started spewing what I thought was cola. Well, I never said anything because my friend was beyond broke and really needed the scratch. Thing is, he made some smart investments and now he's completely rich! It's been a couple years now...should I ask for my money back?

A: Okay, this one hits home. I used to traffic in human organs. Nuthin' big—a kidney here, an eyeball there. Well, this yahoo gave me a sob story once about needin' a liver on the house. Don't tell nobody, but I ain't made of stone. So I slip the slob the liver. Then I find out he owns stuff like a boombox and plates and he's even got a bathtub at home! And Richie Richface is askin' me for a gratis liver? So I go to the apartment he lives in, smash him over the head with a frozen turkey, and take his fridge. What I'm sayin' is, you gotta do for yourself. Go to your pal's mansion, brain him good, pick out somethin' you like, and take it. Happy huntin'!

Q: How do you make the perfect Bloody Mary?

A: A lot of suds slingers are gonna tell you to use some high-quality vodka, tomato juice, lemon juice, Worcestershire sauce, Tabasco, salt and pepper, celery, and maybe even a chilled glass, like you were the king of England or somethin'. It's like freakin' brain surgery. Me, I like to keep things simple. I pour a glass of the nearest bottle of swill and serve it with a ketchup packet. Bottom line: are you lookin' to get blotto or do you want a freakin' bowl of soup?

Q: Yo, Moe! What's the meaning of life?

A: Life is an overflowin' garbage bucket filled with heartbreak, ugliness, crapola, and rage that gets tossed in your face every day you step out into the world. But every so often, somethin' good happens: someone you hate trips and breaks his face, you win a free slab of ribs, that longshot bet you made at the cockfights pays off...and it's enough to keep you goin'. I'm not sayin' it all works out "even Steven," but it ain't all bad either. Even though life spends most of its time standin' on your throat, eventually it's gonna give you a backrub. You wanna get through? Focus on the backrub and not your crushed trachea.

...MOE'S TRIED AND ALMOST SUCCESSFUL* PICKUP LINES!

Babe, you owe me a buck thirty-nine: you're so hot, you curdled the yogurt in my fanny pack.

Darlin', standin' next to you does the impossible...it makes me even uglier.

Well, you're obviously an angel, so I guess your wings got amputated, huh? Did God kick you out for stealin' or somethin'?

Your daddy musta worked at Ikea because you are put together nice!

Finally! You're here! I ordered a tall drink of water an hour ago!

Wow, I never thought I'd see an angel in a craphouse like this.

(Or if you wanna get a good look at her rack...) Baby, mind if I put some breadcrumbs down your blouse, 'cuz I am lost in your eyes.

Can I buy you dinner? You obviously like strappin' on the feedbag.

Honey, it's all right if you got a temper, 'cuz I can take a punch.

Listen, gorgeous, if you're lookin' for an easy mark to seduce and steal his identity...I'm your man.

Holy God, I shouldn't even be talkin' to you. It's like a disfigured rat chattin' up a unicorn.

Baby, you need a "YOU ARE HERE" sign on your forehead 'cuz I am lost in your eyes.

Listen, do you happen to have a blind twin sister?

I'm not officially a hunchback, but if you find that kinda thing romantic, I'm pretty much there.

Man, I want to be frozen until science can discover a way for men like me to have a chance with women like you.

Wow, if you were, like, a type of factory or somethin', you'd be an oil refinery...because the word "fine" is in it.

Now you are a girl worth puttin' on deodorant for.

Hey, if you Spring for me, I'll Fall for you. Please don't hit me.

What's your sign, baby? Mine's "No Fat Chicks."

Baby, watch out! You got so many curves you're makin' me carsick!

Why don't you go out with me and confuse everybody who believes in Natural Selection?

You're so sweet, there oughta be ants crawling all over ya.

Can I buy you a drink? It'll help you tolerate my face. And my voice. And my smell.

Wanna go out? I know I'm ugly, but you ain't no Sharon Gless yourself.

Hi. Please don't mace me.

*NOTE. None of these lines were even almost successful. In fact, more than half of them resulted in bodily injury to Moe.

Listen, if you got a mug like a secondhand spit bucket, you need all the help you can get when it comes to the ladies. My advice? Arm yourself! And I ain't talkin' crowbars and brass knuckles. I'm talkin' about the keys to style, seduction, and not smellin' like a hobo car. I, Moe, present to you, schlub...

THE TOOLS OF THE DATIN' TRADE!

"THE ADHESIVE VALET" LINT BRUSH —
To make the quick switch from bartender to "love tender." It's the best at pickin' up peanut dust, pickled eggshell, and Barney hair from your duds.

MONOCLE — If you find that you've been yammerin' on too long about Ultimate Fightin' or the best discount deodorant stick, squint down hard on one of these babies.

PARSLEY — It's no secret I can't afford much in the way of fine or even sub-fine dining. So I...whaddya call...enhance the places I take my dates to by putting parsley on their plates when they ain't lookin'. Let me tell ya, nothing classes up McNuggets like some fresh parsley!

AFFIDAVIT — With my grotesque features and surliness, dates often worry I might be a felon. That's why I keep an affidavit handy sayin' otherwise.

"GIVE ME A CUP OF TEA AND SOME CLASSIC LITERATURE AND I'M HAPPY AS A PIG IN WARM SLOP."

CUE CARDS — Don't leave nothin' up to chance. Write down some planned chitchat and get one of your bar tab deadbeats to keep it within eyeshot.

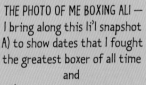

PEPPER SPRAY ANTIDOTE — I can't tell you the number of times I think I'm havin' a nice chitchat with a lady when suddenly I get a shot of pepper spray right in the ol' baby browns. And nowadays, broads are usin' the stuff to stop grizzly attacks... Ergo, I bring along my homemade antidote; it's made of Double-Dairy Krusty Kreamer™, oyster parts, pulverized bagel chips, and fresh rendered horse fat.

THE PHOTO OF ME BOXING ALI — I bring along this li'l snapshot
A) to show dates that I fought the greatest boxer of all time
and
B) to explain the extensive pugging of my nose.

GOODNIGHT KISS NOW!
Ask me how!

COMICAL BUTTON — If I ever make it to the end of the date, I have this little gem to break the tension and send me to Smoochtown! Man, I wonder what that place is like. I'm just so very lonely.

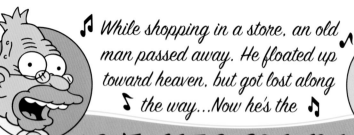

LOVE-MATIC GRAMPA!

Perfect Dates, Perfect Moe-ments!

You wanna laugh? Grab a couple of mugs of cocoa and your best gal and spend a frosty winter afternoon watching drunk people ice skate.

Lookin' for an evenin' of heart-achin' beauty? Take your baby tubin' on a moonless night along the Springoveld Nuclear Power Plant discharge channel...it glows with romance! Literally.

The Rickety Hurler old-timey rollercoaster at South Street Squidport makes for a great date—it usually jams up on the last hurl, trapping you and your gal a hundred feet and change from the concrete below. Bring your "A" game and get to work 'cuz she ain't goin' nowhere!

Recipe for a wonderful night of stayin' in: Takeout from Art Carnivore's B-B-Q Pit and three hours of sports bloopers.

Go gourmet with your gal! Try the "Bring Your Own Brats Night" at the Springoveld Mustard Festival.

Try tripling the magic with...the romance of bein' outside on a balmy night! The fantasy of the silver screen! The savage violence of carnival rides! The South Street Squidport "Bumper-Car Drive-In Movie Night"! IT'S LIKE THREE FREAKIN' DATES IN ONE!

20 TYPES OF DATES

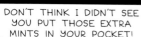

THANKS, MOE!

Sober Advice

to the Somewhat Inebriated

MOE'S *Swingin'* BACHELOR PAD

1. Framed photo of me and Maggie. ("I got a soft spot for that cute little idiot!")
2. Lucky gold-plated beer tap. ("I got this beauty from my Duff distributor for serving my 5,000th beer to my 5,000th customer—Thanks, Barney!")
3. Hangin' noose.
4. Assorted "Plan B" prescription pills – including Sleepitoff®, GoDoze®, and Wait-A-Seconal®.
5. Every issue of "Playdude."
6. 1965 Jayne Mansfield calendar. ("Why buy a new one when every few years the days are the same again?")
7. Tango and Cash.
8. Vase with plastic flowers. ("I like to dress the place up a little to impress the ladies.")
9. Pseudo-satin Playboy Robe. ("We bachelors gotta stick together—right, Hef?")
10. Tube of anti-itch cream. ("Looks like I got a little allergy to Pseudo-satin.")
11. Computer. ("A single guy's gotta meet the ladies somehow. It's either MySpot or 1-800-SEXMEUP.")
12. Phone bill – with $458 in 1-800-SEXMEUP charges.
13. Mad money.
14. Gas stove. ("You'd be surprised—it's not so easy to off yourself in an oven.)
15. Can of Easy-Off™ Oven Cleaner.
16. Bed of Elusive Conquests. ("One time I thought I got a couple hooks undone on Edna Krabappel's bra, until I realized I was yankin' on a spring.")
17. Movie library. ("To keep Maggie entertained when she comes over, I got all 'The Godfather' movies. To keep me entertained when she ain't around, I got the complete collection of 'Chicks Show the Darndest Things.'")
18. Inspirational art.

Every man needs music to set the mood if he should be so lucky as to trick...er...I mean, entice the opposite sex back to his humble abode. These are the records that have worked best for me, especially when played after several drinks and with the lights turned down low. (For some reason, the ladies seem to prefer it that way.) Eat your heart out, Hugh Hefner, 'cuz you got nothin' on...

MOE'S SWEET, SWEET LOVIN' LP COLLECTION!

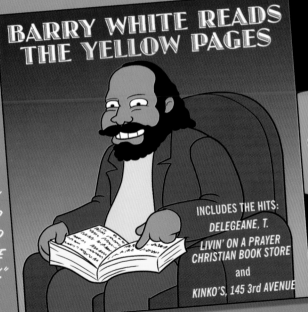

BARRY WHITE READS THE YELLOW PAGES

DO YOURSELF A FAVOR AND DON'T MISS BARRY'S OTHER CLASSIC WORKS, INCLUDING "BARRY WHITE READS TO HIS KIDS" AND "BARRY WHITE READS A COOKBOOK."

INCLUDES THE HITS:
DELEGEANE, T.
LIVIN' ON A PRAYER
CHRISTIAN BOOK STORE
and
KINKO'S, 145 3rd AVENUE

Larry Flynt: My Way
A Tribute to Sinatra

PUT ON LARRY'S VERSION OF "STRANGERS IN THE NIGHT" — WHO KNEW TUNELESS GURGLING DROVE WOMEN SO NUTS?!

DON'T ASK ME HOW, BUT THIS RECORD WORKS.

FLAVOR FLAV: CRAZY B!%@#ES LOVE ME!

SOMETIMES A FELLA NEEDS A LITTLE HELP IN THE ROMANCE DEPARTMENT. YOU GOT A PROBLEM WITH THAT?

PLAY THIS ONE BEFORE YOUR LADY FRIEND COMES OVER TO LEARN ABOUT ALL HER WHAT-ZITS AND HOW-ZATS AND WHOA-NELLIES.

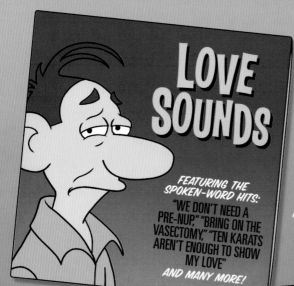

PLAY THIS AND SHE'LL MOVE IN THE NEXT DAY... SO BE PREPARED FOR THAT.

NEED I SAY MORE?

WHO KNOWS WHAT EVIL LURKS IN THE HEART OF THE SINGLE MAN'S FRIDGE...? WE DO! COVER YOUR NOSE AND BEHOLD WHERE THE WILD (FUNGI) THINGS ARE...

MOE'S BACHELOR REFRIGERATOR!

1. 3 cans of Defibrill-Dew "energy" drink.
2. Pack of 12-year-old Marshmallow Peeps.
3. Jar of potato butter.
4. Condimush™ – the all-in-one condiment sauce. ("Now with malt vinegar!")
5. Forgotten diamond engagement ring inside oyster (circa 1993).
6. Gagbury™ egg-flavored chocolate.
7. Fish filleting knife.
8. Lasagna-In-A-Jar™.
9. Bottle of baseball glove-scented sunscreen.
10. Three bottles of Donut-Ade™.
11. Tube of athlete's foot cream.
12. Pancake balls in light syrup.
13. Spare set of house keys.
14. KrustyBrand® "I Can't Believe It's Not Powdered Milk" dehydrated cereal powder.
15. Six-pack of new Pepsi® Bleach with teeth-whitening action.
16. Spare "AA" batteries.
17. Funky Maize Toe Corn Patches™.
18. Package of Bald Eagle Beef Jerky™.
19. Uncle Flem's Brand® Cough Syrup.
20. Blood squibs for Halloween costumes and faking own death.
21. Ace of Mace™ canister.
22. Leftover slices of turkey, stuffing, and cranberry pizza from Pizza Face Pies.
23. Bottle of Kerry's Own® Waffle Syrup & Go-Cart Motor Oil.
24. Hardened piece of Maggie's birthday cake.
25. Box of Cluck Henley's All-Purpose Egg Powder™.
26. "CSI: My Hammy" Bacon Strips™.
27. Yoplait® Steak 'N' Egg-flavored yogurt.
28. Package of Duff Stadium Franks™. ("Now Snout-Free!")
29. Yak sausage links.
30. Open can of Bloated Pig Pork & Beans™.
31. Orowhat?® Grilled Cheese Bread. ("The only bread with the taste of grilled cheese sandwiches baked into every slice.")
32. 96-oz. Espresso-flavored Squishee™.
33. Bowl of unfinished Apple Cores & Marshmallows™ cereal.
34. Six-pack of Eliot Spritzer Canned Wine™.
35. Grandma Fishkin's Old-Fashioned Chum Bars.
36. Cans of Gluten Tag! Barley-Free Beer™.
37. Lovely Rita Pita Maid Brand® Hummus.
38. Opened bottle of Barney Gumble Vineyards® Chardonnay 2003.
39. Funky Cold Medina Cocktail Mix™.
40. Leftover Krill's Jr.® "$12 Dollar Triple Crawdad Burger."
41. Tin of Suri Lee Brand® Famous Bat Brittle.
42. The Desperate Fisherman Seal Sticks™.
43. Fake Easter egg (containing Fat Tony protection money).
44. Tequila-Battered Taco Balls™.
45. Cube steaks, Vodkicles, and Panda steaks.
46. Bag of frozen turnip fries (curly-Q style).
47. 97¢ Store "Mash Surprise" ™ frozen dinners.
48. Corn dog potpies.
49. Frozen toast.
50. Cooler containing spare kidney.
51. Pack of frozen pigeon patties.
52. Mother's Christmas fruitcake (used once to knock out a hungry burglar).

1. Pin Pals League Championship 2nd Place trophy. ("Second place is for losers...Boy, that was a night for the books!")
2. Arson kit. ("This always comes in handy during tax season.")
3. "Bed-in-a-Bag" emergency kit for lady visitors (unused).
4. Stolen mini soaps and shampoos (collected from hotels over the years).
5. Late-night Sin-a-max movie collection (various titles include "Lady Pirates of the Caribbean: Dead Woman's Chest" and "The Devil Wears Nada").
6. .45 Magnum. ("Nobody takes nuthin' from me, and believe me, I got nuthin'.")
7. Good goin'-out shirt.
8. Good goin'-out pants.
9. Good goin'-out socks.
10. Good goin'-out underpants.
11. Pin Pal bowling shirt.
12. Work aprons.
13. Festive seasonal work aprons. ("Them rummies drink more when I get all decked out for the holidays.")
14. Bow tie rack.
15. Springfield High School letterman jacket (earned letter in Varsity Towel Snapping).
16. Funeral/court suit.
17. Picture of Marge Simpson.
18. Hookah. ("I used this during my ol' Swigmore University days—them Indian bongs pack a real punch.")
19. Unfinished novel.
20. Work shoes.
21. Good goin'-out shoes.
22. Authentic didgeridoo.
23. Stolen Springfield Isotopes mascot head.
24. Bowling ball bag (holds bowling ball).
25. Other bowling ball bag (holds keepsake Lucite ball containing former pet Chihuahua).
26. Third bowling ball bag (holds head of beloved sparring partner "Chi Chi" Higuera).
27. Case of Krusty-Brand® Cough Syrup (leftover from the Flaming Moe craze).
28. Not-so-secret floor safe.
29. Combination to not-so-secret floor safe.

MOE'S BACHELOR ART WALL OF FAME!

A classic image on velvet of one of the great entertainers of our time, posin' as some singer.

This is one of them posters from the olden days, when Duff was first made from the leftover washtub water of some whiskey-drinkin' cabbage-lover across the pond.

Ah, a classic! "Dogs Playin' Strip Poker." I can't help but get lost in thought sometimes wondering who won this game...

I don't get the big deal here. It's just a buncha losers sitting around talking to a guy behind a counter. I just can't relate at all.

I ain't never seen this movie, but the poster is pretentious enough to give off an artsy-fartsy vibe, which people take to mean you're all cultured and whatnot.

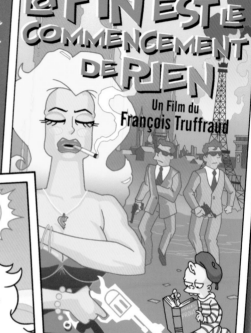

LA FIN EST LE COMMENCEMENT DE RIEN

Un Film du
François Truffraud

Here's a nice black-and-white print of two people in love. It shows you got a romantic side. Chicks usually love that crap, but so far they just roll their eyes and make that cluckin' sound with their tongues.

Every guy's gotta have at least one classic rock 'n' roll poster. I ain't so sure about havin' to stare at a naked guy with angel wings, so this one's best hung in a dark basement or maybe the guest bedroom, where your freeloadin' nephew does nothin' all day but listen to his headphones with a towel stuffed under the door.

LED-ZEPPELIN

College Degree

Springfield Institute of Technology and Internet Poker

MOE SZYSLAK

I bought this at a garage sale for three bucks. It shows you got an education. Or at least that you know how to buy one dirt cheap.

THANKS, MOE!

Sober Advice

to the Somewhat Inebriated

POETRY IN MOE-TION

I am a beer tap,
An empty vessel through which beer flows,
Like blood from my veins.
Good thing that Duff delivery is due tomorrow,
'cuz tomorrow after tomorrow after tomorrow…
I will be all poured out.
Note to self: Order more beer tomorrow!

I never say "No" to a woman
who still has all her teeth.
It don't matter what she looks like.
Neck wattle. Uneven boobs.
Pockmarks.
(I'm talkin' about those real big
ones that look like golf divots.)
That's fine by me.
But she's gotta have teeth.

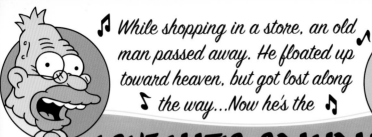

LOVE-MATIC GRAMPA!

Behind the Bar

1. Ol' Faithful. ("For breakin' up fights, collectin' deadbeats' tabs, and keepin' Barney away from the beer truck on delivery day.")
2. Ol' Reliable. ("When they're too drunk to get scared off by Ol' Faithful!")
3. Tipsy McStagger's Freeze-Dried Mozzarella Sticks™. ("For when customers start threatenin' to go home 'cuz they're hungry!")
4. Krusty Brand® Peanut-Flavored Processed Food Nuggets. ("I buy the high-sodium style, so they get their recommended daily supply of thirst-inducin' salt.")
5. Cheery mugs. ("For my regular rummies.")
6. Computer. ("No one can accuse Moe's of not steppin' into the 21st century! I use it to order bar supplies and surf the information superhighway for info about chicks.")
7. Caller ID box. ("So's I can catch that freakin' prank caller!")
8. Men's room key. ("Available only after the two-drink minimum.")
9. Pickled eggs. ("The jar on the left is for VIPs. That other jar on the right is for regulars.")
10. Mini-fridge. ("This baby pays for itself...if ya know what I mean.")
11. On tap. ("The finest varieties of Duff Beer!")
12. The State & Federal Safety Handbook. ("Every bar has to have one of these on the premises at all times. I ain't sure why exactly, 'cuz I never read it.")
13. First-aid kit. ("According to this guy I know, The State & Federal Safety Handbook says I gotta have one of these around, too.")
14. Bar towels. ("From wipin' puke off bar stools to soakin' up puddles of blood on the pool table, where would I be without 'em?")
15. Stainless-steel sink. ("Y'know, when one of them fancy business-men orders martinis with pearl onions in 'em, and my fingers start stinkin' like the onions?...Well, I rub my fingers against the stainless-steel for a few minutes and the stink goes away. It's true! It's called 'ironside-zation' or somethin'.")
16. Lost & Found box. ("It's The Land of Lost Toys, boozer-rendition. This is what's in it right now: Gucci shoetree, tube sock, sweaty headband, The Macarena CD, heady sweatband, Boy George Pez™ dispenser, Vote Quimby button, Impeach Quimby bumper sticker, Blackjack chewing gum, Blackjack playin' cards, a blackjack, Bart's comet, Homer's Odyssey, Lisa's sax reed, and a plastic baby's arm holdin' an apple.")

THE MANY MOODS OF MOE

ANGRY   DISGRUNTLED   PEEVED

SURLY BITTER IRASCIBLE

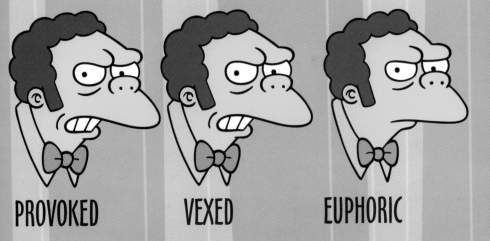

PROVOKED VEXED EUPHORIC

20 TYPES OF DRUNKS

Loose Cannon

"I Love You, Man" Guy

Bar Stool Warmer

Mr. Tall Tales

The Downer

The Smuggler

Sir Weeps-a-Lot

Lightweight

Prankster

Car Accident Waiting to Happen

Captain Queasy

Saturday Night Teaser

Buzz Kill

Balladeer

Freeloader

Gasaholic

Illegal Alien

Ladykiller

The Indentured Servant

Mr. Happy Feet

THANKS, MOE! Sober Advice

WHAT'S GOT YOU CRYIN' IN YOUR BEER, VAN HOUTEN?

ᶜSNIFFLE: I HAVE A CRUSH ON THIS GOOD-LOOKING GAL WHO WORKS IN ACCOUNTS RECEIVABLE.

SO, HAVE YOU TOLD THE BROAD HOW YOU FEEL?

THAT'S THE PROBLEM. LAST WEEK I CONFESSED MY TRUE FEELINGS, AND NOW SHE WON'T EVEN GIVE ME THE TIME OF DAY.

WISE UP, CHUMP! FIRST OFF, GREAT-LOOKIN' DAMES *NEVER* GIVE YOU THE TIME OF DAY. AND SECOND, WHY DO YOU WANT TO KNOW THE TIME OF DAY ANYHOW? YOU GOT A TRAIN TO CATCH OR SOMETHIN'?

BUT I REALLY, REALLY DIG THIS CHICK, MOE. HOW DO I MAKE HER LOVE ME?

LISTEN, PAL, YOUR CRUSH IS BUILT ON FANTASY, NOT REALITY. YOU WANT REALITY?

TRY FOLLOWING THE BROAD AROUND A COUPLE OF WEEKS. SEE WHERE SHE GOES, WHO SHE SEES, WHAT SHE DOES.

to the Somewhat Inebriated

STALKING? ISN'T THAT KINDA CREEPY?

NAH. SHE GETS ON THE UPTOWN BUS, YOU GET ON THE UPTOWN BUS. SHE GOES TO THE GROCERY STORE, YOU GO TO THE GROCERY STORE. SHE GOES TO A MOVIE, YOU GO TO A MOVIE.

IT'S JUST LIKE GOIN' OUT TOGETHER. ONLY YOU AIN'T TOGETHER. SEE?

WOW! THAT'S CLOSE ENOUGH TO A ROMANCE FOR ME! THANKS, MOE!

JUST MAKE SURE IT'S NO CLOSER THAN 500 FEET, ROMEO. THAT'S THE LAW.

LOVE-MATIC GRAMPA!

♪ While shopping in a store, an old man passed away. He floated up toward heaven, but got lost along the way...Now he's the ♪

WOOF! I'D LIKE TO BARK UP *HER* TREE. WHAT SHOULD I SAY TO HER?

TELL HER SHE'S BUILT. TELL HER SHE'S GOT *ALL THE RIGHT PARTS.* TELL HER SHE'S GOT A *RED HOT RACK.*

EVEN *I* KNOW I CAN'T TELL HER *THAT.*

WHY NOT? IT WORKED FOR *ME!*

From the creator of the world-famous "Flaming Moe" comes the latest booze-tastic concoction sure to sweep the land and contribute to countless hookups, hangovers, and how'd-I-get-home-last-nights! Moe Szyslak proudly debuts...

the MOE-JITO

MMM...I FEEL SO SOPHISTICATED.

IT'S JUST LIKE "SEX AND THE CITY," ONLY WITHOUT THE GOOD SHOES AND THE HUNKY MEN. OH... AND THE SEX.

How to Make Your Own Moe-jito!

4 mint leaves, crushed
1 mint leaf, uncrushed
Lime juice (a couple good squeezes on a lime should do it)
A smidge of powdered sugar
2 shots of white rum
2 ounces of club soda
A splash of Moe's "secret ingredient"

So, whatcha do is throw the mint leaves into a tall glass (one of them Collins-style, fancy-pants deals), then squeeze the lime juice over that. Add your powdered sugar, and then crush the bejesus out of it all with a spoon handle, spare nunchuk, or any other thin, polelike device. Then you add your ice, pour the rum over that, and stir. Top off your glass with the club soda and just a touch of my secret ingredient (which'll bring a taste of old Cuba right to your taste buds)—plantain juice! For this, simply take a couple of those stumpy-looking, black banana thingies, throw 'em in a blender, puree into a fine paste, then plop it into your glass there, give it a little mix, and **BOOM!**—you got yourself an authentic Moe-jito! Happy drinkin'! And don't be drivin' no car or nuthin'.

When the regulars drink themselves into depressed stupors, Moe breaks out the humorous beer-blotters to liven things up again!

MOE'S CUSTOM COCKTAIL NAPKINS

AW, DON'T BE MAD, HONEY! AFTER ALL, I WAS CELEBRATING OUR ANNIVERSARY.

DON'T FORGET:
WHAT HAPPENS IN THE CLOWN CAR
STAYS IN THE CLOWN CAR!

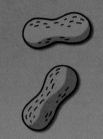

OH, HI! NO,
I WASN'T DOING ANYTHING
IMPORTANT.

TAKE A MEMO, MISS JENKINS! SEND TWO DOZEN WHITE ROSES TO MY...ER, AH...BEAUTIFUL WIFE IMMEDIATELY!

EXCELLENT, SMITHERS! YOU'VE COME OUT AS A GREAT BIG FRUIT.

AT LAST! WHERE NO MAN HAS GONE BEFORE.

"I HOPE YOU DUMMIES HAVE LEARNED YOUR LESSON! NOW, LET ME OUT OF HERE.

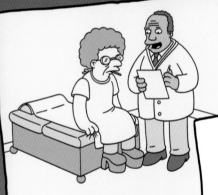

JUST AS I THOUGHT... YOU HAVE DISCO FEVER.

WELL, MAYBE YOU SHOULD GET YOUR SIGN REPAIRED!

Moe's

REMEMBER: *Drink at Moe's to Forget!*

The Flaming Moe - The drink that made Moe's Tavern famous...for about half an hour. The secret ingredient is cough syrup. Well, it ain't secret no more.

Buzz and Fuzz - Made with sugarized, caffeine-enhanced Buzz Cola and Boozer's Choice Brand Peach Schnapps. Put some hair on your tongue.

Downward Sliders - Watch what happens when you substitute the water in a Jell-O™ shot with grain alcohol. (Gulp!)

The Colada Margarita Daiquiri Martini - Something for everyone. Comes with directions to Springfield General.

The Virgin Colada Margarita Daiquiri Martini (Yeah, right.)

Zombie Kamikaze - Drink this and you'll wish you were dead.

Scotch and Sofa - What Groundskeeper Willie drinks— half a bottle of rotgut whiskey. Take it straight up and you better lie down.

Russian Roulette - Imported Welldrinkski Vodka and whatever we squeeze out of the bar rag.

Hibbert Wallbanger - It'll knock you out. Served in a syringe.

Springfield Thunder Bowl - Eight different types of booze mixed with a hint of fruit flavoring in an exotic ceramic pot. Don't swallow the paper umbrella.

Dinner at Moe's - Six beers, pickled egg, and a bowl of nuts. Conversation extra.

Designated Driver - Actually, it's an empty Tiki mug. I got no use for you people.

Signature Cocktails

MOE'S TAVERN
Carries a Full Line of Duff Products

Duff Lite - All the great alcoholic effects of real Duff so you'll hardly notice how watered down it tastes. Drink a lot of it!

Duff Ice - Arctic spring water, Norwegian barley and hops from concentrate, and liquid hydrogen make this the most refreshing taste that ever burned your throat.

Duff Brown - Deep, rich, full-flavored, and hardly sludgelike at all. Use a spoon!

Dennis O'Duff's Private Tub - The cream of the crop. Crisp, pure, deliciously drinkable. Your liver will thank you.

Duff's Hard Fruitade - Made with 10% real juice and 90% genuine liquor. The alcoholic drink that kids can accidentally order.

Duff Nuthin' - The nonalcoholic Duff. For you sissies who can't deal with what's real.

Fudd - Duff bought out a competitor to perfect its cheapest, strongest brew. The beer to drink when you really need to drink a beer.

NO LONGER AVAILABLE SINCE IT BLINDED THOSE HILLBILLIES.

AND NOW, THE GRUDGE REMATCH YOU'VE BEEN WAITING FOR! BELLY UP TO THE BAR, ALL YOU BINGE DRINKERS, AS TWO FOES GO TOE TO TOE TO SEE WHO'S THE BETTER BARTENDER! *OH YEAH!* IT'S...

OWNER AND SOLE PROPRIETOR OF MOE'S TAVERN IN SPRINGFIELD.

GRADUATED FROM SWIGMORE BARTENDING UNIVERSITY WITH TOP HONORS.

EXPERT JELL-O™ SHOT MAKER.

WITH THREE KINDS OF ALCOHOL, A RANDOM SOFT DRINK, AND ANY SORT OF FRUIT, HE'LL WHIP UP A TASTY CONCOCTION.

CARRIES A DOZEN MUGS OF BEER AT ONCE TO A BOOTH WITHOUT SPLASHING.

POURS A MUG OF BEER WITH ONLY THE SLIGHTEST OF FOAM ON TOP.

CLEANS ASHTRAYS, WIPES SPILLS, AND STOMPS RATS WHILE MAKING CHANGE FOR A DOLLAR.

IS CRABBY WHEN HE GETS IN A MOOD.

DESPITE HIS GRUFF EXTERIOR, HE'S REALLY A HUMANITARIAN AT HEART AND WOULD EMBRACE THE WORLD IF ONLY IT WOULD ACCEPT HIM.

...MOE vs. TITANIA

PART-TIMER AT JUGGERNAUT'S HOLLYWOOD WHEN SHE ISN'T HEADLINING AT POLE POSITION: A GENTLEMEN'S CLUB.

ONCE ACCIDENTALLY ENROLLED IN CANINE OBEDIENCE SCHOOL.

EXPERT JELL-O™ WRESTLER.

"WHIP UP A TASTY CONCOCTION" DOESN'T MEAN WHAT TITANIA THINKS IT MEANS.

SPLASHES A LOT OF BEER ON HER T-SHIRTS.

COWORKERS SAY SHE HAS LITTLE MORE THAN FOAM UP TOP.

JIGGLES, WIGGLES, AND GIGGLES FOR A DOLLAR.

IS MOODY WHEN SHE GETS CRABS (INSTEAD OF SHRIMP).

HAS BIG BOOBS.

POETRY IN MOE-TION

Does anyone see me
as I truly am?
Can anyone appreciate the
Moe inside me?
Who am I kiddin' here?
My soul is a dung heap,
A cesspool,
A landfill of rat crap, dog-eared porn
...and broken dreams.

Am I seeing stars?
Are those angels?
Is that the white light all those
out-of-body-experiencin' chumps talk about?
Aw geez, looks like I forgot to blow out the pilot
light again.

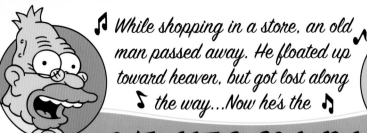

LOVE-MATIC GRAMPA!

♪ *While shopping in a store, an old man passed away. He floated up toward heaven, but got lost along the way...Now he's the* ♪

YEAH, I'VE SEEN IT **ALL** TENDING BAR ALL THESE YEARS.

OH, YEAH? DO YOU KNOW HOW TO MAKE A GRASSHOPPER?

ONLY GOD CAN MAKE A GRASSHOPPER.

DO YOU SERVE COLD DUCK?

I'D SERVE ANYBODY.

WHAT DO YOU GIVE A THIRSTY SKELETON?

A BEER AND A MOP.

YOU **HAVE** SEEN IT ALL.

1. The Chick Magnet.
2. Vanity hood ornament.
3. Navigation system with comforting human voice.
4. "Baywatch"-red bathing suit seat covers.
5. Classic rock laser light show headlights.
6. Auto-eject seats for backseat drivers.
7. NFL-sanctioned pigskin convertible top (also available in MLB baseball glove, NBA basketball, or Texas Hold-'em poker felt).
8. Convenient hideaway barf bucket.
9. Fuzzy dice breathalyzer.
10. Greased Lightning rotating blade rims (for fast and furious street racing).
11. Combination steering and roulette wheel.
12. NASA-designed hover jets to fly over traffic jams.
13. Mood-reading exterior paint (activated by touch to match driver's mood).
14. Environmentally-friendly, beer-converted fuel tank and removable party keg.
15. Hot tub trunk.

NOT PICTURED

16. "**AHH-OOH-GAAH**" horn.
17. Bat compartment (for late-night mailbox baseball).
18. Pamela Anderson-shaped gear shift.
19. George Foreman Grill in glove compartment.
20. Digital dashboard readouts (showing mileage, fuel, and up-to-minute sports scores).
21. Plasma screen floorboards with satellite TV.
22. Wood-fired pizza oven.

HOMER'S MAP TO A BOYS' NIGHT OUT!

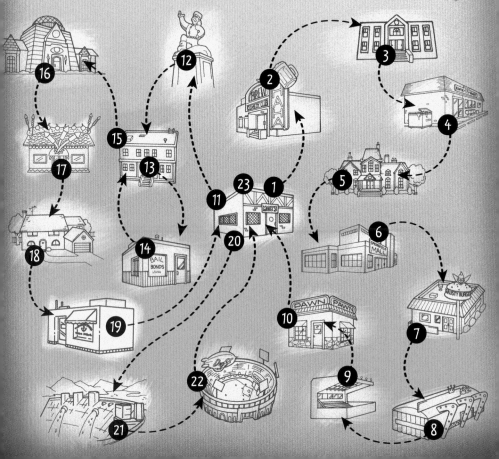

1. Moe's Tavern—"The launching pad of all good blackout adventures!" **2.** Brew-Ha-Ha—"Where the standup comics are always funny thanks to the 4-drink minimum." **3.** Springfield University—"TO-GA! TO-GA! TO-GA!" **4.** Kwik-E-Mart—"A quick stop for money at the only ATM in town that pays in $1 bills." **5.** Maison Derriere—"The perfect place to get rid of all those pesky $1 bills." **6.** Springfield Mall—"To spin a few quick, tire-squealing donuts in the parking lot. Mmm...metaphoric donuts!" **7.** Krusty Burger—"We stop for a little snack. Krusty Burgers aren't the best-tasting, but later on, the extra grease will make them come back up easier." **8.** Barney's Bowl-A-Rama—"Pin Pals RULE! Woo-hoo!" **9.** Springfield Dogtrack—"Stupid 550-to-1 odds...who knew a horse named Stubby Tripsalot would come in dead last?!" **10.** Pawn Shop—"We sell car hub caps and Carl's wedding ring for more money." **11.** Moe's Tavern—"We drink until we forget about losing all our money and Carl forgets selling his ring." **12.** Monument of Jebediah Springfield—"We stop to admire the graffiti of a local artist named El Barto. Lenny says his use of Rustoleum Colonial Red is exquisite." **13.** Springfield Police Station—"Barney gets arrested for 'Indecent Exposure to an Inanimate Object' for mooning ol' Jebediah." **14.** Barry's Bail Bonds—"We get the money to bail out Barney by selling the deed to Moe's Tavern that we took from the display case over a urinal in the men's room." **15.** Springfield Police Station—"Barney rejoins the team." **16.** Stonecutter's Lodge—"We stop in for the ritual sacrifice (every third Wednesday of the month)." **17.** Fireworks, Candy & Puppies—"I buy some M-80s for Bart, some gummi snacks for me, and a chew toy for Maggie." **18.** Evergreen Terrace—"We fire Bart's M-80s past Ned Flanders' bedroom window. He thinks it's the 'a-porky-lips.'" **19.** Happy Sailor Tattoo Parlor—"We get tattoos of our favorite cereal mascots to commemorate the night. I pick the talking bird with the stripey nose." **20.** Moe's Tavern—"Last call. We replace the deed in the men's room with some scribbles on toilet paper. You can hardly tell the difference!"

21. Springfield Dam—"Carl remembers he sold his wedding ring and tries to kill himself by jumping off."

22. Duff Stadium—"Me, Lenny, and Barney run around the bases in our underpants. I slide into third base and quickly realize my underwear came off when I slid into second!"

23. Moe's Tavern—"Closed for the night. We decide to sleep in the doorway until he reopens. Still in our underwear, we wake up before anyone can see us and make the Walk of Shame to our homes!"

STARING INTO THE VOID

MOE'S JOYLESS DVR GUIDE TO TELEVISION'S VAST WASTELAND

⚠ **WAKE UP AND WATCH TV** (30 min).
Join host Edie Banal as she makes a pot of coffee and watches "Oprah."
2 P.M. OUT-OF-WORK CHANNEL

◉ **SO OVER** (30 min). Contestants try to identify washed-up celebrity guests.
2:30 P.M. LOSERVISION

◉ **HMO HOSPITAL** (60 min). Awakening from his coma, Deke learns from Dr. Dirk that he is not dead yet.
3 P.M. COUCH-TV

◉ **WOE, DUDE!** (60 min). A pathetic parade of personal misfortunes.
4 P.M. TRAGEDY CENTRAL

◉ **UNDER THE WEATHER** (30 min). A dreary look at tomorrow's weather.
5 P.M. CHILLIN'

⚠ **ALL TALK NO ACTION** (30 min). A bleak look at today's bad news.
5:30 P.M. ASAP

◉ **THE GLOOM ROOM** (60 min). A depressing look at today's top headlines.
6 P.M. FAUX

◉ **THE DAY IN DEFEAT** (30 min). Sports roundup.
7 P.M. LOSERVISION

○ FRIDGE FULL O' MEMORIES (30 min). Those green, fuzzy leftovers— pets or pestilence?
7:30 P.M. GRUB-TV

❗ IT ALL FITS! - Docu-mental (60 min). JFK, still alive on a Greek island, discusses the
"single bullet" theory. 8 P.M. THE CONSPIRACY NETWORK

❗ THE GOLDEN GUYS (30 min). Herb's latest bout with incontinence lands him in hot water.
9 P.M. SEE BS

○ HONK IF YOU'RE HOME! (30 min). Hijinks ensue when a young couple is priced out of the
housing market and forced to live in their car. 9:30 P.M. HOUSELESS TV

○ GET HAPPY (60 min). Army Specialist Hapman is pinned down by sniper fire. Meanwhile,
the President goes for a bike ride. 10 P.M. F'DUP

○ BOXING FIGHTING PUNCHING KICKING & BITING (60 min). 11 P.M. BADSPORTS

❗ OUTSIDE THE ACTORS STUDIO (60 min). An actor punches a photographer in the nose.
12 A.M. EGO

○ POSTCARDS FROM THE HEDGE - Made-for-TV movie (2 hrs). A woman, finding herself
trapped in a loveless marriage, takes up topiary only to find herself trapped in a maze of
shrubbery. 1 A.M. LADIES CHANNEL

○ STAY UP AND WATCH TV (60 min). Host Babs Dulles makes a ham sandwich and watches
an episode of "HMO Hospital" that she taped earlier. 3 A.M. INSOMNIA CHANNEL

○ LORD KNOWS - Religion (60 min). Packing tips for The Rapture. 4 A.M. PRAY TV

○ SPRINGFIELD UNLEASHED (30 min). An up-close and personal look at neighborhood
weirdos. 5 A.M. PUBLIC EXCESS

○ SMELLY JOBS (30 min). Dumpster diving. 5:30 A.M. OUT-OF-WORK CHANNEL

"IT NEVER ENDS"

Episode 16906

OPENING CREDITS

ANNOUNCER
Like the cleaning of a house... It
Never Ends. With Gabriela DeFarge as
Gabriela St. Farge. Allegra Hamilton
as Sister Bernadette <u>and</u> Roxy
Monoxide. Special appearance by Tony
Vivaldi as Professor Galloway. And an
extraspecial appearance by Margarita
Angelita as "The Contessa." Also
with Moe Szyslak as Dr. Tad Winslow.

INT. TAD WINSLOW'S OFFICE - DAY

How come I don't get a "special appearance"? I'm "special!"

GABRIELA ST. FARGE sits in a chair next to a desk. She wears
designer sunglasses, a diamond necklace, and a plain hospital
gown. DR. TAD WINSLOW enters holding a clipboard.

TAD
Well, Gabriela, what seems to be
the problem?

GABRIELA
I don't know, Doctor. I can't
sleep. I can't eat. All day and
night all I can think of is... you.

She approaches TAD seductively. *Oh yeah. She's hot!*

TAD
I see. Interesting. Well...
according to your chart, you suffer
from short-term memory loss. And you
haven't paid your bill.

Can we put this on the clipboard to help me remember it?

Gabriela reaches for her expensive imported handbag.

GABRIELA
Here's my checkbook. Take what you
need.

Real checkbook, or prop?

Dr. Tad pockets the checkbook. ←

GABRIELA (CONT'D)
But please, Dr. Tad... what about √+
what I need?

She sidles up to him. Tad looks at the chart again.

I like! I like!

TAD
Well... according to your chart, you
suffer from short-term memory loss
and you haven't paid your bill.

Funny idea. Must remember to do this at the bar.

Frustrated, but not realizing the repetition, she digs into
her purse again.

GABRIELA
Here's an envelope full of cash. √++
It's for you.

He pockets the money.

GABRIELA (CONT'D)
And so is this...

She lowers her gown. She stands naked before him.

Can we do this on TV? If so, can we do it a lot?

TAD
Interesting. But according to your
chart, you suffer from short-term
memory loss and you haven't paid--

Gabriela grabs the clipboard and throws it to the ground.
She forces herself into Dr. Tad's arms.

GABRIELA
Don't you want to examine me, doctor?
I need to be examined... all...
night... long... √++++++++++++++++

TAD
Of course, you're right. Step
into my examining room...

Smooooth.

INT. BEDROOM - SOON AFTER

Please tell me there's no stunt double!

Gabriela and Tad are lying naked under the covers in bed.
They are drinking champagne in a post-coital snuggle.

Remember to look up meaning.

GABRIELA

That was wonderful, Tad. You're an
excellent doctor. And this Blottinger's
Sparkling Wine is delicious.

Sounds like a commercial. Do I get more money?

TAD

It sure is, Gabriela. Blottinger's
is the "champagne" of sparkling
wines. And it's now available
without a prescription at your local
supermarket at club store prices.

Is this a conflict because I sell a different champagne brand at the bar?

GABRIELA

Blottinger's. Even I can remember
that name. Which reminds me, Tad,
What's wrong with me?

Tad holds up a clipboard.

TAD

Well... according to your chart, you
suffer from short-term memory loss
and you haven't paid your bill.

Note to self: Shower on day of shooting!

GABRIELA

Oh, well, you can have my diamond
necklace... Oh no! Where is it?

She feels around her neck but it's gone. Tad looks over to
the dresser where it sits and he casually sweeps it into a
drawer without Gabriela noticing.

TAD

We'll have to call the police. But
first, let's look at your chart. I
see you suffer from short-term me--

Suddenly, the bedroom door is flung open and ROXY MONOXIDE
enters. She is glamorously dressed and holding her miniature
poodle, Poopsie.

I hate that actress! They dont call her Roxy for nothing!

ROXY

Ah ha! I knew I'd find you two together!

GABRIELA

(GASP) Roxy! How did you know!

I hate that dog! They dont call him Poopsie for nothing!

ROXY
Because you told me you were coming over here to get your test results.

Am I still naked during this?

GABRIELA
That's right. I came here to get tested because I thought I might have a sexually transmitted disease.

Four lines in a row that aren't mine! Can I take a nap during them?

Tad quickly scans the clipboard.

TAD
Test results...?! Where are the test resul--

Suddenly, the bedroom door is flung open again and PROFESSOR GALLOWAY enters.

PROFESSOR GALLOWAY
Ah ha! I knew I'd find you three together!

ROXY
(GASP) Professor Galloway! How did you know?

Remember to act surprised and nude during this scene!

PROFESSOR GALLOWAY
Because I told you I was coming here to deliver Gabriela's test results.

Man, I've been there!

TAD
Well, don't hold out on us, what do they say?

PROFESSOR GALLOWAY
They say--

Suddenly, the bedroom door is flung open a third time. There stands... THE CONTESSA.

MUSIC STING.

Can we get him to do a concert at my bar?

COMMERCIAL BREAK

♪ *While shopping in a store, an old man passed away. He floated up toward heaven, but got lost along the way...Now he's the* ♪

LOVE-MATIC GRAMPA!

HEY, PROFESSOR, WHY THE LONG FACE?

I AM AS GOD MADE ME WITH THE TEETH AND THE HAIR AND THE ≥FLAVEN≤...

NO, I MEAN, YOU LOOK UNHAPPY.

OH, WELL, BEING IMMERSED IN MY WORK, I DON'T HAVE TIME FOR CLOSE ENCOUNTERS OF THE ROMANTIC KIND.

THEN WHAT *YOU* NEED IS TO SPEND SOME TIME WITH MY *LOVE TESTER*. IT'S GOOD FOR WHAT AILS YOU.

HMMM.

NO, THANKS. I HAD A RELATIONSHIP WITH A GUMBALL MACHINE THAT ENDED BADLY WITH THE SHOCKING AND THE BURNING AND THE NOTSONICE*LADY!*

≥PHEW!≤ THAT WAS CLOSE.

POETRY IN MOE-TION

Dr. Seuss, Mother Goose,
These were the tales
of my youth.
Huck Finn, Holden Caulfield,
Their yearnings touched
my teen-aged soul.
Then I discovered **Playdude,**
And I ain't read
nuthin' else since.

Go to sleep, there, Maggie.
Go to sleep, you little idiot.

Dream sweet dreams, Maggie.

Dream of peppermint candy and
puppy dogs
And winnin' at the track
And calendar models with no

clothes on...

Don't think about how much your
no-good father owes me on his
bar bill or how he stiffed me on
that Super Bowl bet three
years ago...
No, you just sleep now, little Maggie.

Sleep like you don't know nothin'

about how the world works,
you cute little idiot.

THANKS, MOE!

Sober Advice

to the Somewhat Inebriated

Moe's Bottom Forty

1. PEOPLE WHO GET THEIR KICKS STOMPIN' ON A DREAM.
2. RESTRAINING ORDERS.
3. HOLIDAYS.
4. BROAD DAYLIGHT.
5. IRONY.
6. MIXED DRINKS.
7. TRUST.
8. HOPE.
9. FAITH.
10. SCIENCE.
11. TEETOTALERS.
12. 12-STEPPERS.
13. BLOATERS AT THE SQUIDPORT.
14. THE 7-10 SPLIT.
15. CUSTOMER SATISFACTION.
16. FAMILY TOGETHERNESS NIGHTS.
17. FUNKY COLD MEDINA.
18. DELIRIUM TREMENS.

19. WEASEL WORDS LIKE "ALLEGED" AND "SUSPECT."
20. HAPPY HOUR.
21. GOOD FOOD & GOOD FUN.
22. LEGALIZED GAMBLING.
23. LEGALIZED IMMIGRANTS.
24. BOY BANDS.
25. HOLY WATER.
26. EYE CONTACT.
27. WET NICKELS.
28. THE A.M.A.
29. COULD'VE.
30. WOULD'VE.
31. SHOULD'VE.
32. TREKKIES.
33. TAXES.
34. MODERATION.
35. MY LIVER.
36. BARNEY'S BEER TAB.
37. AMANDA HUGGENKISS.
38. THE EIGHTEENTH AMENDMENT.
39. LAWS AND THE ENFORCEMENT THEREOF.
40. MANUFACTURER'S SUGGESTED RETAIL PRICE.